10 MISCONCEPTIONS
that favor
DESPOTISM

The XXI Century Dictatorships
in the minds of their victims

José Benegas

G@lileiland 2015

To those, who starting with their minds, do not give up.

"To be governed is to be watched, inspected, spied upon, directed, law-driven, regulated, enrolled, indoctrinated, preached at, controlled, checked, estimated, valued, censured, commanded….. To be governed is to be at every operation, at every transaction, noted, registered, numbered, counted, stamped, measured, assessed, audited, licensed, authorized, admonished, prevented, forbidden, reformed, corrected, punished".

Pierre-Joseph Proudhon

"There is no crueler tyranny than that which is perpetuated under the shield of law and in the name of justice".

Montesquieu

INDEX

Introduction: Two approaches to democracy

This book is the development of the ideas I exposed at the Simposium "Reverting Despotism. Analysis of methodologies and recommendations to reach freedom" organized by Patria de Martí on Thursday 13 March 2014 at West Dade Regional Library of Miami, where I was invited by its Director Julio M. Shiling.

The title of my lecture coincided with the title of this book, though and due to a question of time I could at that moment only describe three of the misconceptions I personally consider that are the basis for the despotism in Latin America. I hereby intend to complete the analysis of the list, a list that could be even longer.

As sometimes the idea of despotism or dictatorship is opposed to democracy, I would like to make clear two or three points in regard of this subject, before going deep into the list of misconceptions.

Nowadays when we ask ourselves if this or that government is democratic or not, the question has at least two aspects, and not necessarily compatible between them. The first is to determine if the authority exercised by the government in question is "blessed" or not, if it is accredited. With the same intention than if we asked the owner of a plantation exploited by slaves, if he has the documents accrediting said property over them.

That first question about democracy is common to any type of authority, either from a monarchy, patriarchy, or any sort of power that intends to be seen as legal. Title and anointing explain in this case the "right" of the ruler's pretension to be obeyed.

The second aspect to analyze democracy is to focus in values rather than in its "titles". That analysis started at an important moment of the political history with Libertarianism, when its supporters gave power the role of a protective service of rights to peaceful citizens. Under that tradition, the government concentrated power to stop aggressors. In this view, we take in consideration to analyze how democratic a government is, that it should be peaceful with them. But in fact, under this view it is requested much more than the logical fact that the government be peaceful towards the governed: it is undertaken that if it is "my" government, it could never be against me. Thus, in this second view, it is irrelevant if the government is democratic due to the titles it invokes to be obeyed (elections), what matters is if it is a government whose actions aim to protect pacific people and those without influence in public affairs.

That is what Aristotle would understand for legitimacy of exercise. According to the spirit of the United Sates Declaration of Independence a government would last as long as people's consent persists, not by the act of anointing itself – as it would be by elections- but the limit would be repudiation.

However, democracy considered as the government for common people is something illusory to a certain extent[1], because the incentives for rulers to consider themselves above people are still significant. Limited power does not work as it was thought it would and this idea tends to expand even in the most libertarian democracies. The identity between ruler and governed is a bit strange and at the end of the day what keeps a government

---

[1] I make a wider exposition about this illusion in the book "Hágase tu voluntad. Cómo bajar del cielo para conseguir un cargador de iPhone" (Your will be done. To come down from Heaven to get an Iphone charger"), Unión Editorial, Madrid (2015).

pacific, that is to say what refrains it to turn into despotism or dictatorship, is the tension that exists with the attentive citizens (the degree of control that government possesses), what limits are established in reality and how effective these limits are. This is the result of certain formalities but mainly the result of the abstract ideas about government that are predominant in that country and the relationships that the government has with the individuals, especially where those political concepts are originated and distributed.

The purpose here is to identify those concepts and ideas that are simple and easy to detect, that are previous to more evident expressions of despotism. The fact that they are incorporated in an oblivious way makes that the jeopardy to come is difficult to foresee and makes despotism arrive almost unexpectedly and thus difficult to get rid of later.

I will try to highlight the true concepts – somehow forgotten or covered by fallacies- of a system that is respectful of freedom.

The bond between the government and the governed is what is essential and in that relationship the ideas that both parties have of their role are vital and play a key role, particularly the ideas that the citizens adopt. The citizens are majority in number, so if what the governed people think about power were not be considered, a government would hardly keep power by the only use of force. That is why totalitarianism needs the mind control of its victims, as happened to Smith, the character of 1984 who is obliged to love the Big Brother.

The ideas about democracy are then divided, in a first place between those who believe that it is a circumstantial majority that blesses a King on one side and those, on the other, that associate it to a Republic, that is not only inoffensive with its pacific citizens but at its service. What I believe is happening now is that the elected king is filling the gaps offered by the misconceptions and then both approaches get blurred.

Even the anti monarchical- to name them somehow- have accepted a misconception that sustains that democracy is absolute as if elections were sacred and not circumstantial expressions of will (as the republicans say) and in consequence considered more important than the governed themselves. I will go back to this point later on.

Nowadays, it is our turn to find out the contrasts between these two conceptions to refine our theories on power and be able to take a new leap in the evolution of constitutional thought. By now, the lack of paradigm communication is hardly noticed and if the problem is not properly laid out, the absolutism is to win the match. So different are these two ideas that if both conceptions were accepted to define democracy, the term "democratic" in political science would be a completely useless element of analysis.

To avoid confusion, I would like to make clear that when I speak of democracy I use it with the same sense given to the term by the Declaration of Independence of the United States, disregarding the other view for considering it as deceitful, illegitimate, simulated and unacceptable, as any other form of absolute government. Let us say that if any language authority reserved the term "democracy" for the absolutist focus, then this work should be interpreted as a clear defense against democracy.

Having said this, what I now intend to do is to point out ten ideas that are rather widely spread in societies that suffer from elected despotisms, but are having their effects, in great measure not only in those countries but in the so – called western world.

In those countries with modern dictators, these ideas were already settled and were reinforced with propaganda. These are suppositions shared by the majority of the powerless victims of these regimes that complain of what they ask, tied up to a model that disappoints them for the result but they support every day.

Some may even say that some of these ideas are not untrue, that some is or are useful, correct or laudable. Even then, my argument that they favor despotism will keep on. So, at least we will have to think how the absolutist effect can be counteracted if we wish to go on thinking things as I am going to lay out.

In conclusion, the question about how democratic systems such as Chavista Venezuela's and all its satellites are, may include:

1. To ask oneself how "blessed" these cases of arbitrariness are.

2. To ask oneself how friendly that government is with the people, their liberties and rights.

3.   Try to answer if perhaps each people have the government they deserve.

This would be the first misconception, a sort of introduction: the "democracy" is not an univocal term. Its senses can even be antagonistic. Its existence or inexistent can facilitate the political discussion of certain subjects or of anything. That "anything" I will call it here despotism, that is what I assume the reader, as well as me, want to prevent.

There is not such discussion about, let us say, parenthood, trying to find something equivalent to illustrate this dilemma. Parenthood is determined by genetics, or if that were the case by a sentence of adoption. A parent is somebody who raises his or her children and tries to provide them with the best, and it is also a parent somebody who punishes them, hurts his self- esteem or makes them support him/her economically.

A normal person will say that in this second case, the children must be protected from their parents. A dictator will say that his parenthood has no limits and has to be respected. A method to distract from the real problem could be to realize genetic tests and reduce the issue to a question of that parentage test.

The difference between these two last types of parents is of the same magnitude as the difference between "democrats". Hereinafter I will try to lay out ten common ways of thinking that are already incorporated in many societies and that favor – even when people believe they are resisting to them- to work for this abusing "democrats"

From revolution to infection:

The so called XXI century Socialism is a despotism that does not originate in revolutions. It occurs by infection. The whole oppressive apparatus would be insufficient without the existence of abstract ideas that are inoculated in the society and that this society takes, accepts and spreads by means of their principal sources of ethical authority. In some cases in the form of new concepts that have no relation with the idea of freedom, in some others by twisted interpretations and empty meaning

Great part of the struggle against these regimes consists of depriving them of their efficiency; ruin those oppressive concepts that make their everyday life easy. Dismember the ideology of that power, especially the part that the victims have believed.

I am not very sure that this infection has occurred due to a Gramscian plan of cultural dissemination. My impression is that it is more a consequence of some important incongruity in the description of power and of that illusion I referred to before and that the rest is simply the development of the incentives created by the system.

First: Dictatorship is physical violence

When Mr Maduro in Venezuela is obliged to take out to the streets his para-police forces to stop the street protests, this means that the dictatorship he inherited from Chavez has weakened, and has encountered a limit where the instinct of preservation of the victims is stronger than the moral and political poison of the regime and that is why they reacted. Time will say if in the Venezuelan case, this reaction is definitive.

In the perfect dictatorship [2] the characteristics are the silence and a wide system of cooperation to violate the liberties based on precise concepts about the authority that the population has incorporated.

At the same time it is organized a beatifying apparatus of power supported by a strong propaganda, but the main capital they have are the ideas inoculated in society and accepted without

---

[2] The creator of the term was Octavio Paz in reference to the Mexican political system under the PRI

consciousness of their falseness and how decisive of the situation they are. We will now talk of these ideas.

The dictatorship of Chavez in Venezuela, was, of course, much harder than Maduro's. The problem is that Maduro is more inept and is at the end of a period of a parasitic economical system destined to undercapitalize and to impoverish their beneficiaries at an exponential rate.

In the same way that slavery did not consist of whipping the slaves, but of the daily and systematic subjugation of them to their owners and the acceptation of that reality with the same fake sensation of safety than a cage can provide and the support of the supposed racial superiority of the owners, in the same way the dictatorship that not start with the punishment. Additionally, when the domestication method was not enough at the plantations, the whipping began.

Hanna Arendt, called "Banality of Evil" to the integration of normal people to a criminal plan superior to them. That is what the Perfect Dictatorship is about, of that Eichmann really mediocre doing his job with a file, eliminating the principal ethical questions that corresponded to his situations and actions, included the most obvious. The Holocaust would be the predictable output that would happen when the violence unleashed in that imperfect horror that was the Nazism.

That is one of the main difficulties: to separate the type of regimes where we have to consent from those we do not have to. An externalization of the lack of freedom, that is to say of the lack consent, is the physical

violence, the total censorship and imprisonment. But almost everything has occurred before taken to that extreme and it is so effective that it is not recognized.

The new dictatorships carry out that previous process with utmost ease and exercise their threat massively through media networks, creating an unsafe atmosphere for pacific people. They nourish from the worst of society, whom they legitimate in their resentment.

They unusually fight against crime, a fact that contributes also to the creation of that feeling of insecurity. But there is not a permanent express censorship as happened in explicit communist or fascist dictatorships in the XX century.

As a general rule, the opponents do not suffer from physical aggressions or loss of their freedom of movement. It is not that these externalizations do not exist but they are not open and recognized because the regime hides his nature as a rule. These dictatorships are evaluated for all which they avoid to say and by the perceptible fear to question, plus the benefits of becoming an accomplice.

Anyway, those things will occur at any stage of the dictatorship because they are intrinsically in the nature of the power outline and the natural development of oppression leads to a reaction at any moment, but this will be the point when the social system of control fails.

There always survive niches of uncontrolled public opinion and the system is highly efficient getting self-censorship by the provision of an unavoidable alternative, between being cooperative with the government and receiving privileges or not help and go through all sort of calamities. Those niches of people already placed as socially undesirable for the government, will be used by the regime as part of the simulation that freedom does freedom.

The interesting question here is the reason of that difference and what makes us describe a regime as despotic when the dictatorship "is not seen" (or as long as it is not perceived) as it happened in other cases.

Political systems as those of Venezuela, Bolivia, Ecuador, Argentina o Nicaragua, openly express against what they call "the neolibertarian system" or more properly, libertarian.

They keep their intention to be the boss, that institutions must be rendered at their feet, that the press must not criticize them and that if people do not recognize their omnipotence and wisdom, and do what they wish, are the enemies of the State. That means despotism and for us it is quite irrelevant if they were elected, bearing in mind that the expression "government of the people" had just the opposite meaning of what these regimes want to achieve.

When they do not hit is because they do not need to, such as the robber when we accept to give him our wallet. The lack of physical violence in these dictatorships is not an expression of freedom, but of obedience, that they are getting what they want with little yelling, we will be why later on.

It is evident that if we are victims of a government we have not "elected" it, and that if we chose it by mistake we do not have to consent the aggression.

The fact is that these dictatorships have turned up in other moment of history and that they are much more efficient than their sisters, that they manage to go through elections and show the electoral favor of the population, affording the summon of auditors to watch the elections. They even claim that these ballot boxes give them the right of property they have over the population. And being aware that a monarchical idea of democracy survives, they give the act of ointment itself a major importance than actual legal governments.

The reason for the absence of physical violence at the system's climax is the same reason why the heat and noise in an engine are a waste of energy, inefficiency. The perfect engine is that that only produces the mechanical strength that makes it move. The difference between the Stalinism or the Fascism/Nazism and these modern despotisms resides precisely in that their mechanisms of control are much more accurate and prevent the rebellion, so they do not need to repress. They take over the incomes and establish a system of complicity translated in the mafia alternative of privileges or reprisals. At the moment of the total control there are in general no shooting, no detentions, only a permanent, silent and effective state of threat, a system of prizes and punishments and the misconceptions that legitimate them. The demonstrations of tyrannical violence are seen only when these systems get weakened.

The true idea is that the dictatorship expresses itself through the overwhelming presence of the unlimited political will, as we shall see in the next chapter.

Second: The Absolute Democracy

The democracy, if considered as a method to legitimate power, is the weakest of all. This is so because democracy is the system that less permits to sustain any kind of arbitrary measure and the reason for this is that democracy legitimacy is based on the idea of self-government.

The sense of mere "anointing" had a later development; it was a conceptual degradation. No remains of that principle of self-government or its correlate that is consent, could be found in a "legitimate" arbitrariness. It is impossible to believe that someone will be unjust to himself. In the irrational event that he were, in any sense, nobody could sustain that he would not have the right to stop being unjust by getting rid of that arbitrariness that he is subject to. Thus, it does not mean that democracy is the panacea, or that it is necessarily just, but by its proper definition, democracy is the weakest form of government, because it is supposed to vests less power in the "representative" government, which have to be by logical need, just.

It is always cleared up that what is important is the concept of "republic" as expressed by Montesquieu and the Federalists. That notion includes all these principles: alternation (terms of office) of government (they have an end), publicity of government acts, separation of powers, individual rights and equality before the law.

These republican conditions are nothing but the natural consequence of upholding something that is the basis for all the Republican System of government, called "Popular sovereignty", which is not easy to sustain. The limits to power is what makes it real and operative. It is "our government", so it is a government that will not act against us. It is "our government", so it is under control and divided, with a system of checks and balances so that power remains to a certain extent, in the governed, avoiding its concentration.

That is why an absolute democracy, characterized for a government that just for the fact of being elected has no limits, is a conceptual nonsense.

Anyway, it is always a form of dictatorship and dictatorships do not have to be tolerated.

When these republican principles and conditions fade away, the battle is lost and the government is not "ours" any longer. At The Federalist number XXXIX Alexander Hamilton especially emphasizes in that concept of "republic"[3].

For example, let us suppose that the government of Nicolás Maduro in Venezuela were a fledged democracy, as he himself affirms with the support of great part of the countries that belong to the OAS. Should the students that protest for no matter what reason let to be killed? Should the congressmen of the opposition allow not to be permitted to speak and to be expelled?

Well, if we arrived to the conclusion that the oppressive regime of Venezuela -who takes advantage of its power of the State and their resources to perpetuate and attack their adversaries-, is a democracy; then, a single conclusion could be drawn, an obvious conclusion for a person with two neurons in operation, and that would be that we

---

[3] Hamilton, A. James Madison J. Jay and Gustavo R. Velasco. El Federalista. Fondo de Cultura Económica. Mexico, 2001

must urgently terminate with democracy, in the same way that the Americans got rid of the Redcoats in the name of the consent.

Democracy has the lowest imaginable power in a political system to legitimate it, not the highest as I said before. It is the most instrumental form government and contrary to the exercise of arbitrary power. Its main characteristic is not the anointment, but the origin of the power that logically conditions its further develop. By origin, I do not refer to the election, I refer to that sovereignty that expresses the ownership of power, the election is a consequence of that. If the democracy turns absolute, it then lacks of sense or justification.

That is why an elected dictatorship, can be a form of democracy for some dictionary, but it can never be legitimate or bind its victims. A dictatorship is a dictatorship, no matter how it was installed and as a dictatorship it must be fought against. A dictatorship established in the name of the victims is completely absurd, and then, if such a thing existed it must be resisted.

The word "dictatorship" comes from Rome, where the dictator was conceded formally with supreme powers. His will was the *dictum* that had to be obeyed. A dictatorship is carried out throughout the exercise of power.

The opposite of dictatorship is the freedom in a system of objective rules to which the will of the government is also subjected to. The opposite of dictatorship is freedom, not democracy. However, the democracy only becomes relevant when it becomes a vehicle of that freedom, where the will is not present, just the law. When there is no dictatorship, the will of the power is reduced to a certain type of problems, whereas in a dictatorship the law is what the dictator determines.

The dictatorship has nothing to do with the origin of the power, only with its purpose and means. That is to say, it refers to the lack of limits not to an incorrect anointment.

The confusion arises from the recurrence of military governments in Latin America during the last century. The word dictatorship was assimilated to a particular form of dictatorial government. The military governments are dictatorships because they have no law, not because they are military o were not elected by voting.

The Roman dictatorships were so of *iure*, that is to say so formally "legal" in its origin, as the elected dictatorships of our days, or even more. The granting of extraordinary powers and the enthronement of the political will as an exclusive rule took place expressly and following the established rules. The Latin American civilian dictatorships of this century take over de facto powers, are obeyed by the judiciary when they should not, also use public funds in favor of their faction when the formal laws do not authorize so, and they chase the opposition making up false situations and invoking false rules. They only take from legality the act that enthrones them.

Once in power, our civilian dictatorships are actual *de facto* governments. Not having been granted the *dictum*, they just take it over and they even deny they are doing it, something the Roman dictators did not do. For these systems, the election is what enables their dictatorships. So they will give elections more importance than anyone.

This situation is not missed for the granting of extraordinary powers through documents called constitutions, which are actually rules tailored to their needs and interest of power. Because, anyhow, these governments want to continue being "democracies" and they keep up appearances with a Judicial system and a Congress. They are dictatorships that hide themselves in democracy and that claim for them all the power. They pretend all the benefits of a dictatorship under the appearance of a democracy. That is what makes impossible that, even in the limited conception of legitimacy of a Roman dictatorship, they can be considered legal governments. They are elected governments and dictatorships exercising factual powers, but not democracies or *de iure* governments. The Chavista constitution is not different from the act of consecration of the dictatorship in Rome.

However it is necessary to underline that the absolute democracy is not a justifiable system of government. If we call legality to oppression, well, let illegality be welcomed. Submission and consent are opposites. Democracy without the sense of consent is worth nothing.

This misconception predominates due to defects in the explanation of what a republic means and what is its ground. The warning about the nature of the State and the republican sense of the political organization is roughly taught and often distorted not to awaken the defenses of the society. It is the great problem of an education controlled by the State.

If the consent is one of the key factors for the legitimacy of a government as sustained in the declaration of the independence of the United States, and as it is implicit in the democratic legitimacy, the lack of awareness is the opposite. There can be no consent if there is no possibility of rejection. It is inconceivable a consent that is obligatory, irrevocable and everlasting. Those who have given consent cannot be requested to consent again when his freedom is at jeopardy.

Governability and stability

From the misconception of absolute and sacred democracy derives another misconception: "governability". Something like the capacity of a government to perform its political program, when, actually, a republican system does not guarantee such a thing and it would not be desirable that it would. Legal governments do not have their own purposes. A program of government which can not resist the institutional filters or the political counterweights, is not, in the beginning, an aim of the system, it is only of the faction that promotes it.

The failure of the political systems in Latin America -that makes them unstable- is very related with the economic failure, due to the intent of manage a centralized ruled production, distribution and prices. State intervention in economy does not correct any problem, even worse, it is what causes it or makes them worse.

During many decades Latin America has been a region particularly unstable in that aspect, due to the disastrous and demagogic policies adopted. Civilian governments without control of public spending policies ended up in inflation, disorder and conflicts. At that moment, during the cold war, the revolutionary intervention by military seeped in. The militaries, in many cases, took over a " making order" role, applying social discipline and sometimes economic order with a nationalist approach, with the exception of the Chilean case, where the economy was allowed to flow and which became the basis for the future institutional organization of the country.

It is beyond the sphere of this work to analyze the exegesis of the proceedings of succession between civilian and military governments. I just mentioned it to show where the alleged value of "governability" and the panacea of the stability of governments come from. A big misconception that seeps in when the *coups d'etat* were brought to an end in the region as a confused reaction to that reality.

The Spanish Royal Academy Dictionary takes the word *governability* as a synonym of "governance" and its definition overwhelms with its inconsistency. It says:

"Art or form of governing whose purpose is to achieve a sustainable economical, social and institutional development, promoting a healthy balance between the State, the civilian society and the market".

But we still have the problem to find out what "healthy" means or when there that "balance" is achieved. Also, how to analyze the mentioned relationship and which are the differences and the real or supposed conflicts between the "State, the civilian society and the market". Finally, where it take place? It seems that it is somewhere, or in a space called "economy", that we know it "develops", as well as a "society" does.

So, we should discard this definition because, to make things even worse, it defines the word by using an intention ("whose purpose is to achieve").

We would better find a definition based on general use. This is my attempt:

"Governability is the capacity of a government to carry out its policies without interferences or conflicts"

This is how it has been understood and used. For example, when a government loses its mid-term legislative elections, it is usually spoken about how much its "governability" might have been affected. It is often said in these cases that the opposition should facilitate the decisions of the government and put aside for some time the power vested upon them by the voters for the "governability". In some other cases, it is said that some denunciation on corruption involving the presidents should be softened or not mention because it could affect the "governability". If a president is considered weak because he lost support, it is said that the problem is that he lacks of "governability". The same happens when there are street protests for economical reasons or of any other nature.

This is a consequence of those periods of instability, because any of these situations led in the past directly to a coup. The militaries did not need to take the initiative, the civilians recurred to them, not only when the presidents were in a weak position, but also when they took a concentration of illegal power, as happened with Peron in Argentina. However, the lesson was partially learned: it was concluded that it was the weakness of the government what had to be avoided and not the breaking of the law.

There are two reasons that show that this idea is completely wrong. The first is that a country does not exist because it is "governed". A government is not a puppeteer, it is an agency that concentrates the monopoly of force for a defensive purpose, it is not the "driver" as a bus driver. A country is not driven, it is the state that is driven, and the state is a tool of the society for very specific matters. The vision of the country as a ship whose destiny is in the hands of the Captain is tribal and does not correspond to reality.

The government has some roles to perform and there are always different opinions as to how it must carry them out. If agreement is not reached, it is good and not bad if a certain policy decision is not taken.

The second reason of this falseness is that for a republic that tries to move away – among other things- from a military government or any other form of dictatorship, the virtue is not that the government can govern, it is actually quite the opposite. The republic establishes a division of powers, the governed gives opinion and debates, what at its turn reduces the government's maneuverability, and that is the result sought. In a republic the virtue is not the "governability" but the "legality".

I do not refer to a subjective legality identified with the will of the power. It is the Anglo Saxon concept of "rule of law", which I will refer to later on. The government is a slave of the rules, its will is unimportant, its constitutional mission is what is essential, not the political specific goals that put into play at elections, in the case he had.

We get rid of coups to not obey, to be free, to enter legality. The continuity of the civilian governments cannot be based on silence, in the necessity to renounce to debate or to the opposition or to allow them to do the same things that the militaries did. The only subsistence that counts is that of legality.

The most "governable" regimes are the totalitarians. But that does not concern to a republic and it does not need either that the opposition in Congress behaves as if they were not. A republic does not need or does not have an interest in that, because they were elected to perform a political role.

The concept of "governability" is associated to the idea of a government that acts as savior and to populism; it has nothing to do with the alleged republicans principles.

Thus, the true idea is that democracy is a non-sacred system, it is through which the notion of self-government is made effective and that is valuable only when it is a tool of individual liberty: The republic is, in some sense, a system of ungovernable nature, because it aims to curb the government. The absence of these disquisitions, favors despotism in great measure.

Consent is the only legitimacy

One of the standards that can be used to assess the democratic or not democratic nature of these regimes is the Inter- American Democratic Charter that, which require specific things to consider a government democratic, in its section 3. They are:

"Essential elements of representative democracy, include, inter alia, respect for human rights and fundamental freedoms; access to and the exercise of power in accordance with the rule of law, the holding of periodic, free and fair elections and based on secret balloting and universal suffrage as an expression of the sovereignty of the people, the pluralistic system of political parties and organizations, and the separation of powers and independence of the branches of government"

Although the different "Chavisms" do not fulfill with these requirements, this method of assessment has at least three problems:

1. It takes the idea that what is important in the system is that the will of the power be "popular", and not its inoffensive character.

2. It disregards the economical restriction as a loss of freedom, that is an essential element of the despotic government. The violations

to section 3 of the Inter- American Chart occur to whom, in spite of being under economic control, are able to enter into the political arena, and compete with the government. The massive loss of citizenship is not mentioned.

3.   It transfers to international legality, that has no counterweights or controls, the sacred authorization to power.

In International Law, we have passed from giving international treaties a merely declarative character to exaggerate its legitimacy, but the organisms and the treaties are still political pacts among governments, whereas the essential in constitutional law is that power be vested upon common people in the form of freedom and not upon distant entities that play a protective role.

One of the clearer pieces we can turn to, to establish the legitimacy of a government, is the declaration of independence of the United States. Their Constitution does not reach that level, whose preamble starts with the presumptuous supposition that it is being sanctioned by the People themselves ("We the People"), creating a power independent of the real consent to replace it for a formal fiction.

The declaration of independence, instead, does not incur in such a pretension and goes straight to the question of power against freedom, not the power against the principle that blesses it:

"...*We hold these truths to be self-evident, that all men are created equal, that they are endowed by their Creator with certain unalienable Rights, that among these are Life, Liberty and the pursuit of happiness..That to secure these rights, governments are instituted among men, deriving their just powers from the consent of the governed. That whenever any form of Government becomes destructive of these ends, it is the Right of the People to alter or to abolish it, and to institute new government, lying its foundations on such principles and organizing its powers in such form, as to them shall seem most likely to effect their safety and happiness. Prudence, indeed, will dictate that Governments long established should not be changed for light and transient causes; and accordingly all experience has shown, that mankind are more disposed to suffer , while evils are sufferable, than to right themselves by abolishing the forms to which they are accustomed. But when a long train of abuses and usurpations, pursuing invariably the same object evinces a design to reduce them under absolute Despotism, it is their right, it is their duty, to throw off such Government, and to provide new guards "*

This formula is permanent and serves as a real standard. It may sound a bit weak to uphold a government, but that is so because we have accepted the misconception that which is important in a democracy (or political system sustained in freedom if we have accepted that that is a form of despotism) is the permanence of governments, not the individual liberties and rights.

However, the popular anointing of the Constitution, even voted since 1787, does not exist in a form that can be said to involve future generations. In its current version, the Constitution of the United States does not even admit the reelection of the presidents for more than once, but its regulations extend to further generations, forcing even the unborn. The anointing is the aspect that has prevailed, and, as is emphasized as a virtue, the United Stated of America has never had a coup (though assassinations has had), what should be really emphasized is the fact that the respect for the individual liberties and property rights has been a priority in the political discourse of the northern country in comparison with the countries with a repeated history of *coup d'etats*, even though we must admit that the United States has somewhere deviated from the original plan. What I mean is, that it is the subsistence of the value of justice and not the will of the constituents what maintains freedom.

The instability that may arise from reinforcing the role of the consent may only be a problem if legitimacy is taken as a synonym of anointing. But if legitimacy is understood or perceived as the maintenance of freedom, it is clear then for a government that to keep legitimacy is the same problem than to maintain peace, respecting and making respect the rights of people, and then it will be just.

Peace and justice are the core of legitimacy and they can not be lost after the election.

On the other hand, if it is understood that democracy is the most solid form to sustain the legality of a government, and that requires more obedience, then it will have to be admitted that it is being used a single word to describe things of a complete opposite nature. My election in that case would be, as I have previously said, to fight against democracy as the most arbitrary method of government imagined.

The truth that responds to the misconception is that there are more reasons to get rid of an elected dictatorship than get rid of a dictatorship that was never founded on the will of the governed. Democracy is the most instrumental method and the farthest from the sacred ever possible.

If there exist reasons to get rid of an imposed tyranny, there are more reasons to end with an elected tyranny.

Now comes a further study of the false idea and it is the absurd that an elected government has not only the right to behave arbitrarily, but to use the proper State to eliminate its competence, and even then the elections would still be called elections. Actually, the will of the people would seep in any case through that systemic fraud. Only a few perceive the distinction between a clean election and one that is not, as if the cleanliness of the game were something accessory, as long as a software manipulated by the despots shows that the cheat result of the elections has validated all the previous acts.

To that system where not even the elections are clean, as when one plays a match in an inclined field, many that are helpful with that system without knowing, use a very functional and benevolent name and call it "advantagism" or "democracies of low intensity". As if one could say "a little

pregnant" or that could be described as a mischief.
Different forms to minimize the unacceptable.

Third: The class struggle

The absolutist regimes such as those of Chavez or Perón (including all the civilians and militaries that tried to imitate Perón) claim to represent the *People* from domestic sectors that threaten them.

The leftists claim to be the *People* even if they get no votes. Their definition on the subject would be that the "People" would be the good guys, identified with the defenseless. In turn, the "no people" would be the adversaries.

The populists are the people's defenders in that previous vision by which the first are victimized, then weak, then governed by the "popular leaders" that exert the force they lack of. They are avengers.

Here again we have another trouble with definitions that are incompatible and used without clarification, so in the end each one speak of or refer to a different thing. Even in the Spanish Royal Academy Dictionary we can see that difference. People is also a synonym of town, village, but when referred to as a group of human beings, this dictionary- that pretends to have the latest word in Spanish- defines for us:

1. Group of individuals that belong to a place, region or country,

2. Common and poor individuals of a town, village.

More political precisions could be made but with this difference it becomes clear that when we speak of legitimacy of a democratic government -because it is the People which govern-, we allude to so many different realities among themselves, that there is not a point of contact between two paradigms that are given the same name.

Let us start by the second definition. By common people. In a democracy with a republican sense, we imply all the people. The rich, the poor, the engineer, the president. Every citizen is equal before the law. The notion of republic is opposite to that of privileges. If there co-exist common people and uncommon people, then there does not exist republic or democracy.

Humbleness in western Hispanic political culture has become a synonym of poverty, though in the concept there is no reference at all to the size of the bank account. What is clear is that this definition refers to poverty. People then are the poor and democracy would then be the pretended government of that sector. And the poor, for the Royal Academy members are "common" people not like "us". There is a fairly obvious bias in that.

This definition is, in that sense, also incompatible with the democracy, by which everyone is supposed to be part of the political process. If it were the government of the defenseless, that would not be a democracy neither for the defenseless nor for the assassins. If people does not include everybody it should then not be said that those who are not part of the people are obliged to obey and respect the government that governs against them[4].

This second meaning of the word is common to the Marxist socialism which considers the social process as a class struggle and proclaims the dictatorship (not the democracy) of the proletariat. It may also include privileged forms of courts or feudal lords where the inequality is alleged but in

---

[4] In classic Greek, democracy were reserved to some citizens, so it was a very limited one. But those citizen were not defined as defenseless, which would deny their character of citizens.

those cases accepted. In neither of these two cases people vote, not even the "common and humble" people, because their relationship with the powerful is of so-called protection. It is precisely the type of subjugation relationship that the populism recreates in a formal democracy with elections.

The idea of class struggle, rooted in today's western collective thought is one of the falsest ideas of my list and its purpose is exactly to found the inequality between the "party", that must settle domination to put an end to the alleged unfairness and the rest, in the name of revenge of the proletariat.

The measuring of inequalities as a result of a "bad distribution of wealth", when incorporated to everyday language, accept this idea, ignoring that a republic, based on equality before the law, democracy, based on a discussion of ideas in all the society, and peace, based on the principle of no aggression, lose their reason for exist, as well as the idea of independence from the judiciary, since "justice" will now be done by the politics.

Before going on, and since this misconception is deeply rooted in society, it becomes necessary that I clear up that my rejection to the idea of class struggle or of a subjugated proletariat in case there exists a true republic (denominated capitalism) is not because I like the population's economical hardships. That is as the socialist dogmatism wants to view it, or as an unprepared reader might see it if he is not aware up to what degree he has incorporated this false idea. My rejection to this misconception is because it does not correspond to reality and because its consequence is the transformation of its protégés into a state of semi-slavery, and because they will be sentenced to lack of social mobility and loss of hope.

The power of this false idea is huge and is expressed with certain naiveté and good manners under the shape of a do-gooder that looks for a "better world". At Amazon the non- fiction best seller book now is "The capital in the XXI century" by the French economist Thomas Piketty. Piketty makes history and compares data trying to determine whether equality increases or decreases in the capitalist world (which is a terrible simplification). He refers to the also false idea of "the trickle- down effect" by which the economic success of the upper strata overflows like in a pyramid of glasses from the top to the bottom, because according to them and many others, if he demonstrates that it does not happen, he would then refute capitalism. But that "trickle-down effect theory" has been formulated by those critical of the capitalism, not by their defenders.

Let us analyze part by part. Piketty compares the realities of western economies in the post-wars era, that is to say, planned economies and above all with a tremendous credit expansion by the association of the state and the fractional reserve banking systems with lenders of last resource. The first thing to determine would be to say how capitalist is the world that he is observing, if by capitalist we understand the non-intervention of the political authority to enrich or impoverish some individuals and a public spending limited to the real defensive role of the state. I mean, to defend the world with armed forces against the mere "evil", is not a capitalist model.

Piketty observes the growing of inequality in central economies, which is something completely useless to observe. He does so because he has rooted the moral prejudice of the class struggle and then his work is altered and thus his conclusions. The "piketties" come first and then the Chavez arrive later.

When a boat with cuban people get to the coasts of Florida, their inequality grows, it does not diminish. That is the capital mistake of this approach. Said inequality is not a problem, on the contrary, it is what it is pursued. I will go back to this in brief.

What is observed in this type of economies is that after tremendous "incentive" programs (political distribution of wealth), all what is observed are a big dissatisfaction and the impossibility of the middle-class to keep up with their life style. Without having Piketty's moral prejudice, one gets to opposite conclusions, inequality itself is not a problem, the problem is when it becomes harder to pursue the same purposes.

The "trickle-down effect theory" is false because the capitalist economy does not behave like that. In capitalism there are not two separate realities such as production and distribution. That arises from the misunderstanding that some economists cause by their theoretical dissection when analyzing the two aspects of a single question. If production is on one side, and distribution on the other, that is so because there is some authority intervening in the economy. The state or the master of the plantation. In a free market economic system, production and distribution take place at the same time. Someone works for a wage. Somebody sells for a price. Both things happen because their implicit and mutual distribution are convened.

The "trickle-down effect theory" makes the opposite mistake. It worships inequality. As if it were trying to say that it is good that the rich get served first. It firstly accepts the socialist mistake that there is a cake and some come first and eat it (I will refer later on to this dogma), and understand that that is good. That is not good or bad, it is simply false because there is not cake at all. Everything is produced, and by producing or manufacturing, somebody (the producer) gets paid, and somebody pays (the purchaser). Every single economic action is remunerated, the difference between one and others has nothing to do with the order in which they bite the cake, but it does with the relative productivities.

Socialism impoverishes just because they assume there is only one cake to distribute and then what happens is at some moment the cake –that the socialists believed that was given by spontaneous generation – is no longer produced.

Everybody tends to imitate what is most productive among their own possibilities, because an economy with no privileges enables that if my neighbor has a higher income because he sells something more valuable employing the same effort than I do, I will try to imitate him. That is why, when there are no interferences, incomes tend to equal. Not because it is someone's purpose to get equal. The purpose is to improve one's own situation.

If we speak using political terms, we will say that in a republic, there is only one social class, the citizen. There are people who are smarter than others, or some that are more or less prepared than others, with more or scarcer resources, but none of these facts are determined by anything else than people's own actions, personal background and the passing of time. Anyone has the right to become a millionaire, but he has to do it without privileges, without the authority using the force to favor him/her or without using the force himself/herself.

Less-gifted people are not at war with those who are the most gifted people, on the contrary, they need each other, specially the first ones need the second ones.

The idea of class struggle obeys the refuted theory of labor/value of Adam Smith and that was continued by Carl Marx. According to Smith, the value of a thing or service is determined by the total amount of labor required to produce it. If that were true, the business owner would then be exploitative, when getting paid a price (surplus value), they would then be keeping some of the labor invested by the workers in the products. But the value and price have nothing no relation with the labor. First there is an opportunity (for example inequality in the provision of fish between a fishing village and one that is not) and later it will justify to join capital and labor to serve that need. Nobody sums up cost and then adds his pretended profit because he would go bankrupt. It will be depend on how much their clients want to pay for that good or service, and that is something he will have to find out and try to be as efficient as possible to combine resources to become a supplier.

A car manufactured by me, which would take my whole life is not more valuable than one produced in one hour by robots of a modern factory. It is not labor what gives value to a product, it is the product which gives value to labor. The other way round[5].

---

[5] For a comprehensive explanation of the value of goods see CACHANOSKY, Juan Carlos "Historia de las teorías del valor y el precio". Libertas Magazine 20 (May 1994) ESEADE.

Populist despotism takes this misconception to the last consequences, keeping for itself the role of avenger. In this I would like to diminish its responsibility a little. It is the Pikettys who give them that role, and enables them to influence on young people's minds who start to consider themselves as if they were the good fighting against the evil. In most cases they end up in politics and accumulate so much power to fight against the rich, that they will be turned into unconscious and corrupt megalomaniac capable of anything. Because with hypocrisy, any false moral can survive. The most dangerous of all is that Mr Pickety can be the kindest and most sincere person of all. He is so distant from the acts he proclaims than the corrupting process of populism is never seen for him and will go on growing flowers and saying hello to his neighbors with a smile.

After these false visions, populism will play the role of avenger and go over the legislative and judiciary, and dominate the press because all of them are asked to stop the vindictive work of the despot.

The idea of class struggle constitutes the central concept of populist domination. There is a majority victim and a minority victimizer and the populist exerts the force for the majority against the minority, though in this vision, it is not a minority but it is strong and victimizer.

The true idea, on the contrary, is the social collaboration among people of higher, lower or similar income that takes place every day in a private economy and without the existence of casts. This reality is easy for us to perceive in our daily life where we come across with people of different economical levels and we interact and make exchanges, without any problem or class action, unless it be produced or created by politics, for its own and personal benefit.

People is not the group of weak of society, unless we think of a dictatorship. I mean it is not for the idea of a coherent democracy. The populist takes advantage of the fantasy and the weakness will be served by the force of the protective despot every time he assaults a group, a dissident or any dissatisfied.

In the only possible democracy as such, majorities and minorities together form that indivisible political group called *People*, where the power lies. The idea that a part of society is the enemy of another is not compatible with that type of legitimacy. The conflicts between enemies are solved through other channels. All conflicts that come up in every society every day, are solved judicially using judicial criteria that have nothing to do with politics. At elections, "People" does not do justice. Democracy is unconceivable as a warlike methodology among different sectors. A citizen is never an enemy of the state.

John Locke defined the enemy in these terms:

Sec. 17. And hence it is, that he who attempts to get another man into his absolute power, does thereby put himself into a state of war with him; it being to be understood as a declaration of a design upon his life: for I have reason to conclude, that he who would get me into his power without my consent, would use me as he pleased when he had got me there, and destroy me too when he had a fancy to it; for nobody can desire to have me in his absolute power, unless it be to compel me by force to that which is against the right of my freedom, i.e. make me a slave. To be free from such force is the only security of my preservation; and reason bids me look on him, as an enemy to my preservation, who would take away that freedom which is the fence to it; so that he who makes an attempt to enslave me, thereby puts himself into a state of war with me. He that, in the state of nature, would take away the freedom that belongs to anyone in that state, must necessarily be supposed to have a foundation of all the rest; as he that in the state of society, would take away the freedom belonging to those of that society or commonwealth, must be supposed to design to take away from them everything else, and so be looked on as in a state of war.[6]

In conclusion, we belong to a same political base because we are at peace. The "social injustices" as collective injustices and the transfer of rights that will happen during the political process are not a form of political institutional but of a warlike conflict.

If the idea of the war against the rich and the capitalists carried out by the "elected" is accepted, then, at least, elected does not represent those who did not vote them and then they are not obliged to respect their will. One is not a slave for losing elections or not being part of the "proletariat class".

---

[6] LOCKE, John, Second Treatise of Civil Government, Capítulo III.

Fourth: Social Democracy

"The control of the production of wealth is the control of human life itself"

Hilaire Belloc

In the XXI century, the despotisms of socialism are usually identified with neo-marxism.

But this is a big simplification. Even though the alliance with marxism is evident, they all join in a shipwreck where the absolute power allows them to carry out all their whims and grab all the resources. The relationship between Cuba and the Chavism is adoptive.

The true evolution towards despotism starts with a misconception called social democracy. I know that many anti-Chavist or opponents to similar regimes are or consider themselves as social democrats, but there is no other choice than to point out this relationship, and as I already said at the beginning, if somebody prefers to confirm this belief, at least it should be seen up to what extent the concept of citizenship has been destroyed by turning the state into a breeder as a consequence of this square circle called social democracy.

It is usual that an authoritarian government be called fascist for assimilating it to Mussolini's party and to totalitarian despotic practices. But this word is used and was also used by the communists, who, in matters of oppression and slaughter have greatly surpassed fascism. Western journalism has become used not to interfere with communism. I do not know if this is due to a sympathy for a thought that may be they do not know, or simply to avoid the communist diatribe, that form part of the oppressive technology of the Castros. In any case, the appellative "fascist" as a synonymous of despotism acted as a protective shield to hide the horrendous crimes committed by the regimes identified with marxism which, only by the effect of propaganda, was placed in the extreme conceptual opposite. The idea that fascism was an extremist expression of the "right" was generated as well as communism was the extremist expression of the left. In consequence, what was the most opposed to fascism? It was the left. It is a conceptual trap -

though a bit clumsy- because there is no aspect where these antipodes are verified, but it worked well for them.

Now, communism as such disappeared. In Latin America, there persists a more indefinite version of it comprehended under the word "left" and a political expression known as populism. These are people who take as dogma to be better, more idealistic, with the right to order in the name of all the weak of the world united, against all those "others" really victimized by them. Their destiny is to protect those weak who according to them suffer injustices from others who coincide in a hundred per cent of the cases with those who oppose or criticize the so called "protectors"[7]. They are deeply in favor of nationalization and friends of the apparatus of tax collection. It is what remains in common with fascism, marxism, and social democracy: the tax collection funds.

Firstly, this movement is not a marxism because it is not within the category of established enemies of

---

[7] I highly recommend the article "La izquierda hispana: un retrato negativo de la Iglesia Católica" by Cesar Vidal at LibertadDigital.com

the marxism: the capitalists, but only those capitalists who are not their partners.

Neither the internal enemy is defined by the alleged exploitation, but by the dissent. So, they seldom reach the end of the process that supposedly concludes with the exploitation that is the nationalization of the production means. Companies are only nationalized when they fail, just to spread the bad consequences of their policies in the hole society. Before that, they assign business to front men and accomplices, under pressure, extortion and privileges. Populism is hardly a moving tool of a "them and us", a sectarianism by which, anyone who does not let them steal, lie and destroy the economy in peace, is an enemy of all the goodies united and as such they have to be repudiated. A "being good" that makes money by an illegitimate way and that if they has to be the exploiter, in marxist terms, they has no problem at all.

So stupid? Yes, so stupid, because its success is not intellectual, but merely political. They are under the disguise of an "ideology", that I insist is not marxism, is not the product of any book but the result of the public budget and of the convenience of those who colonize the state and provide public education. It has not a precise content and its methodology consists in creating confusion. Its format is entirely proper of Goebbels, that evil genius of the Nazi propaganda, who advised to handle ideas at the lowest individual level possible of intellectual development and whose thinking describe in great measure the usual type of relationship between these despotisms and society.

Good and bad guys is the simplest option. Social control is carried out through this conceptual fracture. The division is never the consequence of anything possible to describe beforehand, because that would mean giving too much independence to their own servants, who only have the option of being attentive to the official channels for the diffusion of beliefs to find out who they must hate today. It is possibly, as happens in 1984, Orwell's novel, that today is the turn to hate somebody who used to be loved until yesterday.

Populism is a pure and hard despotism very similar to fascism, because nationalism is another of its non-marxist elements. But contrary to the Italian movement, the dictatorship of the XXI century, as described by former president Hurtado from

Ecuador[8], is called democratic for having been voted for the first time. The second and successive times are unfair elections, because they use the state to leave competitors out, favor their own men and reduce a great part of the population to serfdom, with the help of another misconception that we shall highlight in brief.

The Latin American left, which comes from marxism, and that has been repeating nonsense during all its existence, is completely in this new business and makes her heir of the fascism. They have been much worse than fascists for humanity, something so they should not consider this insulting. Besides, it is increasingly ridiculous that those who are embarked in fascism, are also engaged in calling fascist to anyone who opposes them for not being so.

The only element that remains from the original marxism is the class struggle, because it is the weakness of those who are going to be avenged what is needed to perform the business. Therefore, the falsehood of this idea needs some clarification. If we speak of marxist ideas, as it is the case of the

---

[8] Hurtado, Osvaldo. "Dictaduras del Siglo XX. El caso ecuatoriano" Paradise Editors (2012)

class struggle or the dependency theory, the relationship exists. But these are misconceptions that lay in society and even in parties that do not consider themselves as marxists. The marxism which is behind the populism is the same that is present in the parties of the opposition, it is not that it should be expected only in the communist parties.

Cuba is an ally of the Venezuelan regime and if nowadays, after a very long process, we can say that they both form part of the same single political reality, the substrate of concepts behind the populist breakthrough, comes from the social democracy. The communism as such is still rejected by the vast majority of the population.

The social democracy gave populism, in the name of equality, a little importance to rights, and places vital elements of the life of the citizen under the tag of "materialism", where there should not exist the same obstacles to state power than in other areas.

It is important to understand the true exegesis of populism, if we do not do so, only their effects will be attacked, without eliminating the causes that can be found in that egalitarianism that fails to explain reality and which constitute the breeding ground for despotism. This will be hardly accepted by many, or most, of the opponents of these regimes that dream with performing a system of general assistance and control of the economy for the political allocation of resources, without the most evident authoritarian characteristics of the dictatorships of the XXI century. But we have to be clear about this issue, this way is not only wrong but it keeps the ambiance where populisms will return once and again and again to take advantage of the incentives provided by that program.

Social democracy destroys the citizen by a double way. It points out the successful companies as being a problem and as if they captured a part of the wealth already created to put it only in their favor and in detriment of the poor. Even though, the social democracy will not run a tough campaign against them as populism would, but once they explain reality as they do, they should. Many years in favor of preaching this division between the good and the bad ones, (identifying the first group with those who do not posses and the second ones with possessing, giving more emphasis to the verb possess than to produce), do create expectations about someone who some day might turn up to put an end to the problem. The producer then represents the vice, turns himself into a culpable citizen and under vigilance.

The second weakening of the citizen takes place on the other side of the population. Those who are explained that they are victims of the ambition of the rich go into de assisted group category, and then become subjects of the state.

The society is then divided into dogs bodies who pay taxes and people farmed that must thank their existence to the mercy of the power. The republican relationship with the state disappears. In the social democracy the liberties get less relevance in the name of said equality.

I will not go into economic considerations, I will only point out that the social democracy vision is incompatible with the citizenship of a healthy democracy. The division of society that they encourage between the good and bad guys places the social democrats in a priestly place. They believe to represent the economic good against the evil. They are persuaded to be more sensitive than the libertarians, the businessmen and traders, whom they see as lost in sin. After that, we only have to wait until a fanatic or thief understands how to use that moral and political substrate in his own benefit.

This false idea leads to failure, and this to populism, which in turn will blame the social democracy for not having deepened its policies based on their explanations of reality.

A common feature of all XXI century's dictatorships and which will help to illustrate this point is the absolute arbitrary use of the economic restrictions of their egalitarian and interventionist policies taken against dissidents or opponents. There are some economic rules that are invoked as an interventionist policy and previously legitimated by the social democracy and used to scourge the disobedient. Those that are favored by these regimes are compensated with subsidies, protections and public works, all tools that are used by the social democracies for an alleged common good.

The silent dictatorships that do not use the physical violence would not be able to exist if the official coercion were not facilitated by the liberticidal economic power practiced in almost all Latin America even earlier than the Chavisms arrived.

The new despotisms admit that it is true what the libertarians sustained about social democracy, that is, the impossibility to divide the liberty in political and economical liberties, and that the restrictions to this second ones are not a simple option of economical policy management, it is the actual aim of liberty. They also knows that its result is not the common good but the creation of a privileged cast in and around power. This is what they want.

The liberty we refer to is political, it is related to the relationship between the unarmed citizenship and the monopoly of the force kept by the state. The right to property, the right to trade, the possibility to dispose of the fruit of one's own work, are political liberties defined in the relationship between the individual and the state. That who needs to ask for permission can never be a complete citizen. It does not matter whether the permit is required to import a product or to speak of a certain public issue.

The social democracy and the interventionism tried to establish a realm of liberty, restricted to politician's own activity, that is not the same than that of the common people, who work, trade and hire. For statism, politics is what counts, because politics is their world, not the economy, which they live of but do not care about. For them, political liberty means generosity and economical liberty, means selfishness. Two categories of people are thus inevitably created: the politicians and the common people, this latter must be protected and consequently guided.

The social democracy tried to manage that question with an egalitarian criteria, but despotism is perfectly conscious of its utility so that the social discipline can be treated as a type of political economy and in case it is useful to them it is precisely because it alters the balance before the law. This is their main weapon of domestication, the reason why businessmen hide themselves, hire institutional relation managers that make them look friendly to the political *statu quo*. Many people, as it happens with the artistic ambiance in Argentina, persuade themselves that the ones who keep them up or condemn them to die from starvation and in ostracism, are their savers. It is the same reason why cowards try to show brave by stoning the undesirable.

The key for the lack of obvious violence, that we spoke of in chapter one, is that this control is performed as interventionism, which facilitates them to get an income and to discipline people.

With the manuals of social democrats and interventionist economy at hand, they decide who will survive and who will not, and with an increasing public spending, they form an oligarchic privileged cast. The regime then will offer as the mafia does with "silver or lead" and it in general nobody will disobey this premise. The majority of the population immediately abandons their civic roles. And this happens so efficiently that we are forced to evaluate all the alleged republican counterweights of all these countries which have almost been reduced to a parody.

I do understand that what I say here leads to a bit uneasy conclusion or may be impossible to juggle with such a wide criteria of democracy or republic, enough to shelter even the anti-democrats. This is why I consider necessary to be precise about two things in particular. The first is that evidently the democracy can not coexist with the anti-democracy. The equality before the law, as proclaimed in the republic and in my opinion, logically supposed in a democracy, is not compatible with the equality of wealth nor with the political distribution of the produced.

The second explanation is even more important. The conditions required for the existence of a true republic are such that the new issue that we have to solve within the field of the philosophical politics is whether the concept of legitimacy of the government is compatible with the idea of freedom, the two aspects that the classical libertarian thought has tried to unite (the ruler identified with the governed), especially throughout American history. My answer is no, but I will not go further on this point[9]. What I express here is that for a republic as it is conceived and has been thought, the political distribution implies its destruction and that has no remedy.

But this does not mean that it does not exist a way to be socialist in a true republic. It actually does but it is not practiced because then, the costs of that being socialist would fall on the socialists themselves and there are not enough fans for that. I mean a type of life in a private community, without using force to impose this type of life to anyone. Kibutz or any other form of community by which the social democrats can show the rest they really believe in the community and the equality of benefits independently of who may originate them,

[9] I take these matters in "Seamos Libres: apuntes para volver a vivir en libertad" (Unión Editorial 2013) and "Hágase tu voluntad: bajar del cielo para conseguir un cargador de iPhone" (Unión Editorial 2015).

and believe in the superiority of this system in relation to capitalism. But I insist, those social democrats do not exist.

It is not possible to use the state to change their wealth and keep on calling that a free form of living.

Of course that there exist the social democrats who refrain from taking the abuse they have helped to happen to its last consequences as the despots do. Afterwards, they end up regretting that the dictators do not do "all the good they could do" because they are unaware that they themselves have opened the door to despotism.

The truth is that which we call "market", which the social democrats as well as the socialists consider harmful, is nothing but an analytical tag used by the economy science to name the network of bonds and transactions that people perform when they are free, when they have rights.

It is a clear contradiction to be in favor of freedom and against the market. The free market is the freedom of the people, the most common and of every day use. In politics the intervention in asset formation and in the exaction of the results of what people do, including those formed with savings, capitals and risk them. This means mutilating the citizenship and their political independence. This is inevitable and Latin America is a perfect example of this reality.

The assumption that the poorest people gain "freedom with a full stomach" due to political power, is one of the biggest fallacies of our time. The assisted are dependent, they unlearn, in the case they had been allowed to learn, the capacity of fending for themselves. The only existent policy against poverty is freedom. There are people who know better how and what to produce and that have the capacity to get capitals to venture in their visionary project. That people needs the other for all they do and those less gifted, with less savings, need them as much as water is needed in the desert. They do not need the politicians who submit them in the name of protection.

Fifth: The equality

This misconception is atavistic, but with socialism it becomes a theory and with social democracy it becomes the basis for the new despotisms.

Republican thought refers to a very specific equality, the equality before the law. This means that we are all measured by the same yardstick and that there are no privileges. The equality before the law is a way to make the value of justice possible.

The socialist equality refers to this axiom that is the moral recognition of the injustice itself "from each other according to their capacity, to each one according to their needs". As I explained in a previous book, being that needs are unlimited, the use of the state power to satisfy those needs, leads to the unlimited power, with no exception[10] (10).

---

[10] "Seamos libres" ibid

This is where the equality in benefits becomes so useful to despotism.

The political distribution of production does not reach other equality rather than in the generalization of poverty, altering at the same time the balance of those who distribute and form a privileged cast. But they do not care, because the purpose of proclaiming the equality is not to reach it, but to get that unlimited power involved in bringing it into play and the authorization for assault in the name of a "being good". Unlimited power, assault, and moral blessing; that is the real (political) business of the equality.

Usually, the French Revolution is said to be the starting point of a libertarian process, but we must be cautious not to get confused and think that the fact of getting rid of the absolute power with a romantic sense, actually produces a liberating result. The most recent experience of Castro's revolution should be enough to understand this. The French Revolution was actually an explosion of resentment and violence that instead of establishing justice, as the American previous rebellion did, tried to carry out the false egalitarian ideal. Instead of putting an end to privileges, the emblem of collectivism was hoisted and the end of merit.

The French Revolution motto expresses the defense of the false egalitarian idea that feeds despotism: *freedom, equality, fraternity*. The fraternity as brotherhood, collectivism, as a moral ban to the individual project, as a denunciation to that who stands out and follows its own path to happiness. Equality in a wrong sense and not as a rule that is fair if it applies to everyone and where each one gets what he deserves and has fought for. Fraternity and equality ended up with freedom and not only did not generate an idyllic world with all holding hands but it created guillotine. So much goodness, requires a raid. All socialist slaughters have been like that.

The Austrian economist Ludwig Von Mises (1881-1973) invented the term "Montaigne 's dogma" to refer to the false idea that wealth is inherited and fixed, so that no one can get anything except that it be at the expense of someone else. This belief is behind the egalitarian ideal.

That denomination refers to another economist, of the XVI century, Michel Eyquem de Montaigne (1533-1532), who on the basis that the wealth is a previously determined stock, sustained that no one can get a benefit without damaging others. Thus, in the exchange there was a winner and a loser. This idea is implicit in much of the political hot air that encourages envy and resentment and this assumption is completely false as Mises himself proved.

In order to exist a voluntary exchange, not a street assault or a tax collection, both parts must obtain a benefit determined by the fact that they value more what the other part offers than what they asked to give for.

If I work for a certain salary it is because the salary is more valuable than my effort, if I sell a certain product, it is because I value more the money I will get for it or the goods I will be able to get with that money. The other party values in the first place more the work I offer than that money and in the second example he prefers the product to the price he pays. The mutual benefit does not only exist, it is also the final purpose of the exchange. The only way by which the exchange is in detriment of one of the parties is that that exchange takes place against the will of one of them, as happens when there is coercion (assault and tax collection).

If we all valued the things in the same way at the same time, trade would not be possible.

Wealth is not that stock to share out, it is something that is produced permanently: The bread we will eat next week, has to be made first, and many exchanges must occur, of people who in his own benefit will carry them out so that in turn we will be able to pay the amount of money we value less than the bread we want to buy. The bread and the wealth do not need of strict politicians but of producers and everybody produces when it is at his own benefit, except that he is subject to serfdom.

The Montaigne's dogma offers a huge benefit to despotism. It provides the energy of all the economic frustrations of society, which are explained by the welfare of one's neighbor. At the same time that despotism destroys wealth and increases that frustration in a vicious circle, he will take advantage from it.

Why equality is never a problem?

The inequality in goods and wealth, in resources and skills is never a problem. It is an anxiety inserted and carried from archaic times, probably from the human nomad era when the subsistence depended on fruit collection and hunting and everybody contributed equally in the group to get that provision[11].

In our present and complex society it does not have any other meaning than the facilitation of manipulation and "in-equalization" of the equalizers.

If someone does not have a house, it is not due to the fact that someone else owns it. That someone else owns a house is not a problem for that one who not has it, it may imply that he is closer to get it, not farther. Something that everybody wants and nobody has is more scarcer and then more difficult to get than something that everybody wants and everybody has. If the percentage of people who wishes a house reduces, the inequality among that part of society that still lacks of it (which is smaller) is bigger, not smaller, in comparison with the rest. Should we consider wrong if the percentage of people who do not own a house diminishes? The truth is that if I am the only one who does not own

[11] See Hayek's "The atavism of social justice"

a house (the most unequal of all), I am closer to get one than if I share that luck with more people.

The socialism that feeds the despotic regimes is not a result of the "social needs" but of a vision of society through envy, through Cain's eyes would be in Adan and Eve's allegory.

The "unequals" in a society with no privileges and no casts (as those established by socialism when created the proletariat), not only do not fight, but they are who have more reasons to collaborate. That is Pikkety's huge mistake. We all need that our clients be richer than us.

With the ominous vision of the classist victimization, when a company establishes in a poor country looking for cheap labor, it is judged as maleficent .

But let us take a moment to observe the mutual benefit, the entrepreneur not only does not reject those who are in the worst conditions, but he goes to hire them. The employees of those countries, with those lower salaries, increase their income, are looked for and take the arrival of the company as a blessing. The consumers of the product manufactured by that Company will also get a benefit. Inequality is what makes that those who are more gifted or skilled to manufacture a certain product, do it for those who are less skilled. The general outcome is a flow of goods and services that are more and more accessible to everyone. The skill of the juggler would mean nothing if it were not for the spectators who watch him astonished because they lack of those skills.

On the contrary, the comparison of salaries between workers from countries with low salaries and those from countries where salaries are higher, is worthless. If salaries were equal, the company would not have moved and the same would happen if the difference were politically prohibited. If that measure were partial, the paralysis effect of the measure would be proportional, in no case and under no circumstances, the political intervention in a relationship of mutual benefit is useful, because when the gap is bigger, the mutual benefit will be bigger too. The company that finds out the opportunity speeds up the moves of other companies and then those salaries, if there are no interferences, will go up faster as a consequence of the pressure of the demand.

Inequality moves to action and it is the action, which narrows the differences. But the purpose is not to narrow the differences, it is the convergence of interests among those unequal to improve their lives.

Nowadays, with the ease in communications and transport that we have, what prevents all countries with low salaries to transform themselves in capital receptors, are the political barriers and above all, the labor legislations which indicate the companies that the salary signal must not be taken into account. Any policy against the inequality of possessions, goods or capital, is a policy against the transference of goods and capital, which would narrow that gap.

It is an impoverishing policy. But this is something that those who support an anti capitalist moralizing do not dare even to consider, which shows that their concern is not poverty, but their own image of inspectors against evil and their pretension to be benefactors of humanity. The economical reality that they prefer to reject shows that their alleged heroism is not worth a coin.

What is also curious is that by narrowing that gap, it opens others but that is not bad news. It was never bad news as the inequality, considered as that information that makes act, has no relationship with the principle of justice except that said inequality were the product of a political decree or of violent acts.

One of the reasons why this misconception is highly accepted is the existence of privileged people who get advantages of the use of state violence. Friends of power, who once hired by the state, get rich because they are favored by politicians or the industrialists protected with customs barriers to their competitors from the rejection of the consumers. Mainly, in the despotism of the XXI socialism which is characterized by an oligarchy, in the strict meaning of the term, defined as that group which dominates the levers of power (not of the economy) and puts them at their service. That is to say, that the privileges that are attributed to the market are completely opposed to the characteristics of their existence.

This is the point where the right idea converts in its medicine. The right idea to counteract the equality of wealth is the equality before the law. This essential concept in a republic indicates that there are no privileges (laws which benefit a certain group) and that we are all governed by general rules, which make no distinction between those who have more or less, whether they belong to a certain stratum or faction or are friends or not of the power. The equality before the law or the equal law for all, makes it possible that the inequality of wealth generates the flow of mutual benefit that we referred to before.

The XXI century socialism alters the balance greatly in that sense. Friends and enemies are treated differently. Friend is the ally, the partner or the accomplice. Under that category of friend of the power, comes the protégé, who plays the role of worshipping the leader, who is the biggest unequal, treated as a superior, wise and infallible being. Of course, in the XXI century socialism or new despotism, it does not exist the equality of wealth at all. Those who are in power and their court, monopolize all the business using and taking advantage of the state and building barriers in order that the private individuals can not act to satisfy their needs and improve their situation.

Sixth: The wise government

Platonic philosophy tinged Western political thought. In his famous Allegory of the Cave, Plato describes an existential situation of a common man and postulates that the society has to be guided by wise men who are able to see things how they really are and not how they are reflected.

This idea has survived up to the present and has succeeded in seeping in the free world even when it is not consistent with the republican thought, as Popper clearly points out in "The open society and its enemies". Let us see why.

In the Allegory of the cave, Plato mentions some people sitting in chairs and looking into a cave. They have no other choice because they are chained at their heads and feet, so that they can only look in that direction. Behind them, the light comes through from the exterior of the cave. At the entrance some things happen whose shadows can be seen reflected at the back. The people chained can only see the shadows but not the reality itself happening outside. One of them is set free so he can see in the direction of the light, which represents God, and see the things as they actually are. This person can never go back to handle his common affairs any more, he is on high, struggling with the problems of the good.

This man is the philosopher and the allegory symbolizes the relationship between the people, who is a slave of his ignorance (identified with the people who looked at the shadows) and the perfect government of a philosopher sovereign.

The ideal that persists up to our days in a form of government and legitimacy opposed to what Plato thinks, is the ideal of the wise government, a government that settles the good and the evil. We should submit ourselves to the will of the best of us. Plato is really explicit on this quote that Popper makes in the first part of the said book:

"The greatest principle of all is that nobody, whether male or female, should ever be without a leader. Nor should the mind of anybody be habituated to letting him do anything at all on his own initiative; neither out of zeal, nor even playfully. But in war and in the midst of peace—to his leader he shall direct his eye and follow him faithfully. And even in the smallest matter he should stand under leadership. For example, he should get up, or move, or wash, or take his meals ... only if he has been told to do so. In a word, he should teach his

soul, by long habit, never to dream of acting independently, and to become utterly incapable of it."

The republic is not based on leadership. The ruler does not guide a society, he only solves some of its trouble and conflicts.

The required wisdom is not general, it is specific on what has to be solved, which in the case of a free society is not much, because the ruler is not a general medicine as the authoritarians think. Those people are not guided *"for that one who knows"*, but they choose, experiment and guide themselves on results, in a dispersed process of trial and error, where those *"who know"* would eventually be able to interpret but never reproduce, guide or create.

In an open society the best demonstrate it permanently in the private world. They are not anointed with a special degree of the "best", they simply stand out. Or may be they do not stand out, nobody can have the acknowledgement guaranteed, as people are free, they are also free not to perceive the value of things or to have an idea of value different to ours. But there is something else that is very clear and this is that in politics it is not the best who stand out, but those who have a better capacity to submit and manipulate the rest.

The problem is that in the platonic world the power has always built its own epic, in a tradition that has no relation with the republican. In that epic, the good is associated to the power.

In the same book, Popper quotes Pericles in contrast with Plato:

"Even though only a few are capable of giving origin to a politics, all of us are capable of judging it"

As I said before, in fact things work the other way round, only the individuals are capable of creating the policies. A few are capable of interpreting and explain them, but not of conducting or replace them. In a republic the government is not a guide; it is a server.

Hayek elaborated a theory opposite to that of Plato which was laid out in *"The use of dispersed knowledge in Society"* [12] that is compatible with the political republican system.

There, he explains why society can not be conducted through a centralized organism. This is because the knowledge is dispersed in the

---

[12] Published for the first time at the American. review XXV, September 4th 1945.

individuals. It is only the affected person, who knows what is specifically more urgent; whether to fix the window in a very cold place or to go and get some food. The circumstantial knowledge that is indispensable at the moment of taking decisions is within people and is not at reach of any elite. We denominate wise to the person who knows of something concentrated, not extended, but is incapable of replacing the rest of people in their decisions.. It is very probable that a philosopher is not even skilled at the moment of handling his life.

The government commands, it is not a question that the ruler has some knowledge on medicine and sends us to have our tonsils operated. That, is something we have to decide by ourselves. The individual who robs our car, by the same reasons, he can not justify his action by saying that he can drive better than us. Because to know or not to know is not the question.

As to the government, the question is neither to know or not to know, but to know when the use of force is justified and the imposition over the rest, because that is the nature of the government. The wisdom does not alter the character of an aggression and in the decadency of our systems of government it is usually argued in a way that an unfair imposition is covered up with the implicit knowledge of the impose.

Hence, the relationship that exists between those who are for the election of the "wise" and the authoritarian thought, even though they can nor reckon it.

Then, the ideal government in a republic, is not the government of a philosopher, it is the government of the just, of the guardian of respect and freedom.

To illustrate this confusion, I remember once when during one of my radio programs I complained about a regulation imposed to the restaurants of Buenos Aires. A lady phoned to ask what I knew about restaurants. The question, however, was not about what I knew about them but to understand the problem caused by making the government guard the most trivial aspects of the social life and not realize that the problem exists. What I know, I answered that lady, is that people can run a restaurant without being helped by any bureaucrat, even more, they can run them in spite of all of their obstacles. All I know is that the entrepreneur not only risked his capital to open the restaurant but that he also knows more about restaurants than I do and that the bureaucrat does.

So, what I affirm here is that the idea of the wise government is false in its pretension to find *"the best guide"* for a society and that this idea has nothing to do with the republican tradition.

I think that the purpose would be to have the most effective ruler in giving security to people and goods and I believe that nothing could be worst to try to reach that purpose than to give the power to someone who believes is above us.

To understand the nature of government and what is referred to when it is asked its intervention, let us imagine the state for one moment without policemen, army or weapons. What remains of what we call government?

Now let us imagine it without tax collection, a state which would have to borrow money from its taxpayers. What would that government be?

So, when we hear someone asking for official intervention, let us bear in mind that what he is asking for, is the use of force and the capacity of getting resources without earning them. Taking them from someone who produced them.

The idea of the populist savior would be the bizarre version of the same misconception. What is worst is that many times, the opposition insists in offering *"true saviors"* instead of the false ones and they criticize the personal defects of the dictators.

Seventh: The State is the Law

In a republic, the law is not any product that comes out of the legislative power. Otherwise, we should admit racial persecution, slavery or censorship, all of which have been part throughout history of formal "legality".

To fulfill the sense of this type of libertarian legitimacy, it is necessary to comply with a condition and this is that we are governed by a principle known as "rule of law". In the Anglo Saxon world, the word "law", refers to the rules of custom consolidated by judicial decisions or precedents. The source of production is different to the codified continental system, that is why it is easy to distinguish the law from simple legislation.

Anyway, the legislation in the continental system is subjected to a constitutional rule and the constitutional rule to the individual freedom, which is what supposedly gives meaning to it. Once again, I know this may sound restrictive, as if I wanted to reduce the republic to my own opinion. But, it is a fact, the division of powers itself has no justification if the state is the source of happiness and not an apparatus of force that has to be restraint to perform a defensive role. If the state is the source of happiness, it is absurd to limit it. Thus, in the only political philosophy where a republic fits in is in that of freedom.

When referring to dictatorships I mentioned before that its characteristic is that it is the will of the dictator what governs and constitutes the law. The meaning of the law, identified with the legislation issued by the competent power, is similar. The law ceases to be something objective to study, resolve and confront with reality and what the parties wanted, to turn into an interpretation of the political will, not in the hands of the dictator himself but through a legislative power.

The Italian jurist Bruno Leoni narrates the origin of the private law in the Roman republic through the decisions of the praetors on cases submitted to their jurisdiction[13]. What we still know as private Law (though nationalized later) was originated in Rome. After that, with Justiniano, those principles discovered by the study of cases were compiled. In a later evolution, there appears the continental

---

[13]   Leoni,   Bruno.   Freedom   and   law. http://mises.org/library/freedom-and-law

method of legislative production through an specific power, once it is understood that the legitimacy of the decisions is given by the code itself and the state which "creates" the law, instead of the disperse production of rules based on private needs.

Hans Kelsen, elaborates an alleged "Pure theory of the law", where the word "law" is identified with a pyramidal legitimacy that starts from a political decision, that is to say the reverse process of that of roman praetors. It is this inversion in the process of production of the law what gives birth to the misconception of this chapter; that is, that the state itself is the law.

If that were true, we would only have to study the words of the legislation to find out the "legislative will" and then apply accurately the political orders whether for the construction of a bridge or for the elimination of a sector of society.

But it is not necessary to take it to the extreme. This way of identifying the state with the law, spreads the legitimacy of the obedience and the conversion of the whole society in herd. About this misunderstanding, the populists only have to climb up to power to settle the square circle, which means the "legal dictatorship" or "legitimate" one.

Montesquieu in "The spirit of the Laws" describes the model of republican formalities. There is the "legislative power", perfectly limited based on the continental tradition.

A problem is then created, because private issues, where the state should not get involved, are automatically incorporated to the political arena. This private issues, may include from marriage, to contracts, all subjects that generate unnecessary controversies every time the society evolutions and people express new necessities in the way they handle their own and personal affairs. The society gets used, in the meantime, that all issues have to debated publicly, including their sex lives.

In that confusion, many people, instead of claiming for freedom, since they do not know that is a chance, ask that the legislation contemplates new situations, such as, in some cases with the state declaring if somebody is a woman or a man or the other way round. The opinion of the state should not count.

In this confusion, too, the legislators, feel themselves as gods, though they are simple despots.

They sit in their benches to imagine all kinds of orders on any issue that goes through their heads. They also hire wise consultants- those capable of seeing the essence outside the caves- to indicate them the sense of their projects of "laws" that will regulate the private sector.

Even more, newspapers quote how many projects of social regulation each legislator has prepared, and turn themselves in "workers of the legislation". A truly stellar nonsense.

In order to prevent populism, we are interested in giving emphasis to the fact that the state is so submitted to the law (the constitution in first place) as any other citizen. Otherwise, we can not speak of a republic, only of a legalized despotism.

On the other hand, to bring down that myth implies to enable a debate on the political activity and the arbitrary pretensions of public servants and magistrates, instead of the permanent subjugation to anything in the name of a false ethics of obedience and conformity.

EIGHTH: The problem is corruption

I could say that this is almost a misconception. Several clarifications should be made here. The first I would say is that in order to the concept of corruption itself exists, there must be a clear idea of correctness. Corrupt is what degrades of its own essence, so that is why we must determine and understand what that essence is before explaining why this idea is on this list.

According to what it was said in a previous chapter, there is a conception of a good government following an aristocratic point of view and another from a democratic, libertarian or republican. There we have two different essences, so different that corruption can not have the same meaning for all of them.

Legality also has two very different senses. One would be the result of the state formal will and the other as the product of evolutionary rules (some will say natural).

Thus, the analysis of corruption should start with those definitions.

Ethics is defined as that which is believed that must or must not be done. It depends also on what one asks oneself or does not. The despotic society has several blind spots for which is fully responsible. I have already mentioned Hanna Arendt's work in the "Banality of Evil". When the pertinent questions fade away, what then follows is an appearance of correctness from people who will set themselves as an example of honesty and in their inconsistency will be capable of doing anything.

In a despotic society the main corruption is not the bribe in the public bidding process, it is the tacit acceptance of the division of the society between dogs bodies who economically support the state and servants, who are supported. It does not matter how real it be the result of this plan, because what actually happens is that they are all dogs bodies of the system. The ethical degradation of the republic system -where all citizens should be equal before the law- rest in that paradigm.

What happens is a reductionism from the institutional ethical to the personal level of the public agent who do not respond totally to the distributing apparatus which distribute social benefits, which is completely functional to the tyranny.

In addition, when the sense of legality is limited to the formalities of the legislative will, the issue becomes more blurred. To give a clumsy example of the formal vision of legality (positivist), paying a bribe to a guard in a Nazi Germany concentration camp, would be considered an act of corruption. For a libertarian vision, the corruption would be the existence of the concentration camp, even though its creation had been voted by the Parliament. The payment of the bribe would be the equivalent to the ransom paid in a kidnapping, which is protected by the fact that it is given under coercion.

Going deeper, we will see that for the social democrat vision, the problem of corruption is taking resources from charity of the state. On the other hand, under the libertarian vision, the corruption is a robbery against the tax payers.

For a nationalist thought, the "privatizations" are corruption and mean the "surrender of the national resources". Under the vision of the libertarians, a "privatization" is simply the exchange of a company for money that is applied to other functions and which enables a company to self-manage it business and become subject to the market risk (if the privatization has been real).

Of course there are acts that are considered corrupt, no matter which the initial paradigm had been. For example the payment of bribes in a bidding process of public works, even if their explanation of the values involved was different. The interventionist will find that the purchase of permits for example, to export tomatoes has to be punished. The libertarian will consider corrupt the mere existence of the permit and will try to abolish it. The authoritarian will find that the society must be guided in a platonic way and that doing something that is beyond of what is permitted is an offense. The libertarian considers that people are free and will fight against the subjugation of ones in favor of others.

One of the problems of these differences is that they are seldom admitted and that when debating, the same words are used to refer to completely different phenomena. If we understood how trade works, we would never accept an increase in customs controls and the mere existence of smuggling (trade against the band[14], against the order, in disobedience) is unacceptable as a crime.

---

[14] A literal translation of the Spanish word for smuggling would be (commerce) "against-band".

For interventionism, its sense of corruption is essential. In the ideal world of heroes, the fallen is the devil. There is a line between holiness and hell. That who infringes upon the apparatus of happiness, legality, ethics and social guidance, being the one who in charge to guide it, is the worst sinners of all.

For libertarianism, the problems of corruption in general are solved through incentives which allow people to reach their aims without the need of permits or demonstrating that one is being "good" to humanity, according to the moral codes of the Big Boss. Particularly with punishment and the recovery of the stolen. But corruption at a great scale will be solved and above all, the corrupt ethics of the benevolent distribution.

If a corruption resulted of the interventionism is inherited, the solution will be political, that is to say, remove the obstacles created by the planners and their effects (which we call corruption) will then terminate.

The idea is false, as it is expressed in the title of this chapter, because the main problem is not the corruption of the police news but the existence of opposed honesty parameters and the ignorance of the problem. In the second place, it is also a constitutional issue, which results in the incentives created as a consequence of the political decisions.

NINTH: The press will make as free

By when the despotic regimes start to attack the communication media and try to establish censorship - either by direct or indirect means,- several things have happened before.

Five years ago, in Mexico, I spoke at the Forum organized by "Caminos de la Libertad" (Roads of Freedom - Azteca TV) about "What we lose when the freedom of expression is lost". My answer to that question was another question: What has already been lost by when the freedom of expression is lost.

Press, as we know, or to be more precise, as we idealize it, as a form of expression entrepreneurially organized, is a product of capitalism actually, not the means by which capitalism was reached.

The history of communication, which starts with rhetoric in Classical Greece, and reduced argumentation, ends up, in a recent period in the press business that offers varied news contents in return of what readers get commercial advertising.

In this era, which we would call professional era, the press is another service of the market and crowded of people of the trade providing the service of telling us what is happening. The opinion is a complement of that service.

The neuralgic point of this business is the company advertising which buy audience to sell their products.

But when the economy changes and it starts to be mixed due to an important presence of the state and when the percentage of income given to the state grows exponentially legitimated by "other economic ideas" and the "protective" vision of the state, then the weight of commercial advertising diminishes its importance. The freedom of any company is restricted by the eye of the state, by the need of showing accounts and giving explanations. And news companies are no exception to that rule.

But I have not analyzed yet the problem of the new dictatorships. This degradation is the inevitable consequence of the importance given to the state with their new explicative and benefactor doctrine and that is when the system- by which the press in the past had developed with independence of the government-then changes.

Let us see the contrast between the Watergate scandal in the seventies and the political standard of inspections carried out by the IRS during the Obama administration against entities or corporations related to the Republican Party and the Tea Party movement. There is a huge difference between the way how the first episode was dealt and not tolerated and this second that was almost unnoticed.

This happens in the country which has reached the highest standards of freedom and however a degradation can be noticed. In all the Western the role and importance of press is changing.

The difference with the populist dictatorship is that this latter not only knows it, it takes advantage of it. They are fully aware of how much a company can be conditioned only by the rules or policies alleged destined to correct the "distortions" of the market. Thus, in the first place, no journalistic company enjoy the same freedom that some decades before. Secondly, it is directly harassed. In the third place, as in these countries the state is the principal advertiser, it takes away all the possible little advertisers from the market, who would not be able to advertise their products if that big "client" had warmed the demand and created a journalistic market at its image and likeness.

That is to say, the professional and guardian journalism is a consequence of freedom, not a cause. Before this journalism, that is to say before the market was a system for the satisfaction of the private needs, there existed other forms of communication with different characteristics.

In these, there was a debate of ideas and political fight, the powerful were questioned and it was fought for freedom as a main concern. I mean leaflets, for example. A piece that does not pretend to provide a service to the market but to show a situation or denounce to whom may hear, but who is not willing to adapt it to what his interlocutors want to hear, producing sometimes without remuneration and editing with resources of their authors. To turn off the market obliges to make the leaflet explicit. I say explicit because as the republics turn into an skeleton which contains a a very different political system, the press and the media suffered the same changes. And when it is said to protect the freedom of press, those skeletons are defended, that are also skeletons, even when they deny or deny themselves the change under the appearance of a neutrality that turns into an accomplice of what is happening.

The road to freedom is not made of that journalistic model that tries to be in the middle between freedom and the attack to freedom. The press as we know it will come back when the freedom wins and not because the communication without freedom is less important, but because the communication to be truthful must not pretend asepsis.

I know it may sound weird that I consider illegitimate what these dictatorial governments call "militant journalism". Because with the wrong exegesis it looks as if the main value is which is defended as "objectivity" but transformed in neutrality. The value in fact is the truth, as reality. If what happens is that a dictatorship is moving forward, the right thing to do would be to describe it, which, in the traditional model of financing turns almost impossible.

So, is it right to be a militant of the freedom and wrong to be a militant of the dictatorship? The answer is that of course it is, there is no possible relativism in this, nor bridges between freedom and dictatorship, they are irreconcilable enemies.

Even the fact that those who are in favor of dictatorship get financing with public funds is another immorality, but the principal immorality, if we have a republican ethics is to defend the indefensible.

One of the great frustrations in the new despotic systems, is that even if there exist pressures and censorship, some things are known, including very scandalous cases that involve presidents. In that sense, Internet is a tool of great help and not in the sense of what is traditionally known as journalism, but because of data that leaks by unexpected ways; unexpected ways that require sorting and discarding.

In Argentina, Mrs Kirchner was laid bare for getting huge sums of money from a contractor of the state, with the alleged purpose of hiring all the bedrooms of her southern hotels. It is known that she and her husband, together with their relatives and friends, were assigned big extensions of public lands of their province –ruled at that time by a puppet- at a vile price.

But even when some media discloses it in the middle of a cross-fire with the government, with serious patrimonial risks and subject to the permanent official diatribe, nothing happens.

The frustration comes from the fact that many people still believe that the single fact that an scandal gets disclosed, produces huge effects. But the Watergate case happens in the United States, in these despotisms, the scandal not only does not surprise but also in the end, it gives the feeling of a huge impunity, which makes them stronger.

That is why the political problem between the free press and the government only takes place when there is freedom. The true idea is that the ink and the brain must be used to fight against despotisms, it is not enough to denounce them. They will never die for bad propaganda, they will survive and by when the means of communication, exhaust them in their possibility of resistance, they will still be alive, and living from what does not belong to them.

Despotism must be deposed to be able to enjoy free press again.

TENTH: Income tax

A great concern about the surveillance kept by the state was caused by the Edward Snowden case, the contractor of the United States's services of Intelligence who denounced that the federal government carried out a general plan of espionage to the population through internet and mobile telephones.

However, nobody seems to observe that the most relevant surveillance started a century ago. Its importance is vital to make possible the new despotism of the XXI century Socialism.

In 1913 a very serious fact for the subsistence of the individual freedom against the state occurred. The problem by which it was unnoticed is one of the consequences of having called "economical policy" to the infringement of individual rights.

I refer to the 16th Amendment of the United States Constitution, by which the federal government gets rid of the restrictions of the verdict of the legal case

"Pollack versus Farmers Loan & Trust Co" (1895), which had declared unconstitutional the income and dividends tax established a year before, for being a direct tax.

After eighteen years of getting used to this idea, the 16th Amendment allowed this tax, which requires for tax collection, a wide system of surveillance over the population.

That this were a direct or indirect tax, could be part of an endless debate, similar to the debate of the "democratic" character of the XXI century despotisms. Because the important in both cases is the engagement on freedom and property, without them, freedom is a lie.

I like to define slavery as a one hundred percent income tax. This means, that no matter what the rate is, that is the degree of slavery that the "taxpayer" would be submitted to.

One could say that this is applicable to any tax and this is true. What makes income tax particularly negative for freedom, is that it reverts things as to the purpose of the state, because now the question will be, not which things should be made with the public budget, and how much it will cost to debate if they are worth doing or not. The question will now be to see how much the dogs bodies produce to establish, afterwards, in what things the state can spend and how powerful the state is.

However, this is not the main reason why I include in this list as false the idea that the state must participate in the incomes of the society as a partner, patron or owner of the population. Surveillance is what is pertinent for this list and the fact that the citizen, who used to be owner and master of the country, is now in the position to give all the time explanations to the state, show his accounts and transactions, his savings in banks, his credit cards, , all of which is inherent to the income tax. That who is under surveillance now is not the citizen that breaks the law or threatens the population, but that who produces. It is him who must show his expenses, his income, and prove them, to do affidavits, be subject to threatens, and criminalized, and if he is not accurate, effective and collaborative with the tax collector he will be severely punished. What is left of a citizen after all that? Very little, actually.

The United States, as I have already mentioned, in spite of these calamities, has a long lasting tradition in cherishing individual freedom and property. This does not mean that these measures do not produce damage, or that they do not have the same effect that everywhere else, but they are slower.

On the contrary, in our Hispanic countries- where that degree of freedom was never seen and where the state has been seen as a giver and breeder of defenseless sheep, the effect for that method of financing the state was devastating. Economically, in not many decades, the amount of tax collection over income grew exponentially. But politically, it turned the population into a flock of sheep.

The high taxation summed up to a high inflation made everybody survive by cheating , because the "legality" turned impossible. Weather the result had been sought or not, it is applied here what Ayn Rand said about the intention of the political apparatus to place everyone outlaw: to choose then the moment to chase us. That moment will come when we become annoying. And in a despotism that happens often.

The government -thanks to the income tax- knows everything about us. In arbitrary countries, the companies are pursued relentlessly by the treasury through inspections which end up with fines determined by interpretations that are always favorable to the state and validated by judges who think that if the state do not get funds, the world will disappear.

The population itself, exhausted, under close surveillance and chased, is persuaded that their enemies are those who do not pay taxes, and make them pay more. They never question the tax collector.

This combination is a *bocatto di cardinalle* for despotism. It has a monitoring and punishment service which uses openly with factious purposes. The companies can never finance any private organization or press media to criticize or denounce the government, or even tell people what is happening. All their movements are watched and if they do not adjust, the state arbitrariness will make them disappear without the need of moving a single soldier or threaten directly.

The companies themselves adjust and adapt and their communication policies turn pleasant, their managers are trained in the absolute amorality, political amorality mainly.

The same happens with both, professionals and population in general, whose silence is observed but we do not understand why, since the system of surveillance did not come out of the Soviet Union, but of the Unites States.

Amid that arbitrariness and an anti-drugs policy, there is a strict surveillance of the cash flow to prevent the financing of terrorism. It is certainly a problem for terrorists and drug dealers, but also for those who struggle against arbitrariness or to finance politicians of the opposition without being watched. Ones and others are in the same bag, those who hide to attack and those who hide to defend themselves or run away.

As I said at the beginning of this chapter, even in the case that one agrees with the idea of the income tax or believe that the state action is wonderful, what can never be denied is the restriction to one's privacy, to move or to act as citizens to resist dictatorships. We have to take care of that consequence.

What is true, is that without income tax or restrictions to the movements of private cash flows, these despotisms had not gone far.

In relation to the fight against money laundering, is a complete nonsense. If the movements of funds have relation with corruption or terrorist's activities, they should be allowed and not prevented, because that would lead investigators to find the authors of these actions. But it is not very clear if they try to prevent them or protect an "onshore" banking system.

As to the persecution of drug trafficking, I leave it out of the list, because in my opinion this is a complete mistake, but I will not expand here on this topic, tough it is related to the degradation of many governments. It would exceed the aim proposed here.

The misconception behind the income tax is really rooted and it will take a long time before it goes under revision. It is extremely important that this moment comes. Nowadays the 90% of the companies formed in the United States fail. On one side, this figure helps to understand that to associate the word company to a world of privileges is absurd. It is also good to wonder how many of them would have survived if a smaller part of their profitability or none would have been used to finance the public sector.

However, the most urgent thing is to understand the threaten involved in the surveillance, control and subjugation given through this type of taxes to despots and to also understand the constitutional and legal measures needed to escape from this peril. I'm not speaking of an assumption, I'm speaking of abuses that are occurring now in the dubious legality we are living in and which allow the XXI century despotisms to practice oppression as if it were pure law enforcement.

So, then, even those who are for egalitarianism and income exaction can understand the threaten and think of immediate solutions. The United States Constitution, in its fourth Amendment, set the principle that the state can not initiate an investigation without a "probable cause", which is applied to penal suits. In their fiscal policy, this principle was completely disregarded. In general, the fiscal persecution takes place in the administrative field. And that must be forbidden. No citizen should have an inspection without a "probable cause" and justified before a Judge in a due process.

At the same time, the discriminatory use of the power of tax collection, inquiry, surveillance or inspection of people for political reasons should be penalized. A criminal offense should include inspectors, clerks and officials who participate in that sort of actions and who know or suspect there might be a political reason to perform them with a long term prescription.

Presumably, the state collects funds to perform its functions and that the principal of them is to protect people's rights. It is completely unacceptable that this sequence begins with the violation of the aim pursued.

CONCLUSION

It would not be of much use if we overcame this revival of the Latin American authoritarianism and were not capable of detecting which are the beliefs that make it possible, because if we do not, we would have, if lucky enough, new governments to replace them which would lack of a clear direction to be able to get out of the conceptual dictatorship the region has been enclosed in for so many decades.

If we enumerated the cases of dictatorships we would find a minority, but the misconceptions herein mentioned are present everywhere, waiting for someone to take advantage of them.

If these ideas were not changed, then the governments to come, would replace the dictators but would leave the authoritarian system intact and would fail, on one side due to a parasitic system which always produces de-capitalization and impoverishment, and on the other hand, and to make things worse, they would make the despots look more determined, braver and with stronger moral convictions than they themselves.

It is not an indulging amorality what puts an end to the ruling of the bandits. On the contrary, it is the pride to sustain an ethics based on peace, the respect for the individual rights, the value of effort and the independence from all sheep breeders.

I believe this is not only possible, I believe this is indispensable. Many believe that "the people" do not want face reality, that they will always be more willing to listen to the demagogues and to prefer to be treated like irresponsible children.

I tend to think that the main problem lies in those who believe that and not in the supposed irrational mass. It is them who think that their burden, that is to say reality, adulthood, seriousness, and honesty is week. It is them and not "the others" who have internalized these false ideas, which led us to this point.

Neither the despots are "the people's parents" nor we, those who reject those despots, must replace them in their role. We are all adults, no matter how big our patrimony is or our academic degree. Thus, this is not about protecting the sheep from the bad shepherds and cheat them with good tricks. What will protect us all is to fight against falsehood. It is hard to find out a big truth, but if there is something really simple in this life is to reveal a lie. Courage is all that is needed.

I do not consider that illiterate or poorer people need to diminish the importance of the property rights as the social democrats or the egalitarians that have incorporated those false ideas.

This paradigm, is alien to the poor. The sense of property is clearer for someone who does not own much than for someone who owns the enough to waste his energy in paying pardons to the social resentment instituted.

Once again, the class struggle or the marxist polylogism - by which our thought is conditioned by the economical position- do not exist. That is a complete nonsense. The stories are the usual resource used by manipulators.

Lastly, my proposal to the reader is to fight despotism in our minds and in those minds who may want to listen to us. Their fall will then be a question of time.

How to stay with despotism

Luckily, despotisms do come to an end. A society that punishes those who produce and rewards the demagogue runs out of an energy which does not recover, it gets poorer and fails, and also degrades morally. This does not mean, as many would expect, that the failure per se would produce changes.

We usually see in these countries how those who try to oppose the despots repeat the same misconceptions that strengthen them, in order to enthrone its own benefactor despot.

They innocently believe that the despot is of evil nature but that they will be good. But it is not so, someone who considers himself a platonic philosopher and places himself in a higher position to the rest to take hand of the resources of power, is a corrupt already, no matter if he smiles when doing it or by trying to save the world.

The savior is corrupt just by trying to be savior, no matter what he becomes throughout time for making a false image of himself. That is nothing but the collapse of a fictitious personality.

The first step not to get out of despotism is to think that the power system can become a real Santa Claus and the problem is that the tyrant does not let be so. Reality shows that the tyrant is not Santa Claus because Santa Claus does not exist, not because hi is not interest in being so. Cynicism is the outcome of an impossible idealism.

Besides, that idealism is unnecessary. Many things can be achieved, progress is possible. That people get out of poverty by themselves and without a tyrannical effort is possible. But that requires of a process, action and time. Such a thing only happens in a constitutional context of rules, and the first of them is that no one will be robbed, and much less for producing.

It also requires to give up magic and bet on adulthood, that means to assume costs in order to get benefits and accept the idea that to get them we must take step by step. But this process is accelerated as capital, as a result of saving, is being accumulated

It is not possible to escape from despotism just by changing people, or with the help of genius with good "technical knowledge". Authoritarianism and meritocracy are like water and oil. There is not such a thing as a good concentration camp guard or a good secretary of commerce, for the same reasons. There does not exist a good socialist judge, no matter if he graduated with honors. The socialist has a sense of justice that is opposed to that of a free society.

We can not escape despotism without a market. This is rather difficult to understand when the lack of division between political and economical freedom has been accepted or when it is assumed that the economy belongs to materialism for having a "guilty" vision of the acts of possessing, wishing, obtaining.

This kind of ethics is despotic, no matter from what angle we analyze it. Freedom means being able to act in one's own benefit without being accountable to nobody.

With no property or commerce (I do not say here free commerce for not being redundant), there is no civilian society possible

With no market which is the (analytical) field where the individuals exchange things without the intervention of the authority, there is no space for any individual independence. Those who have put an end to the market have also put an end to all types of freedom, not because one goes after the other but due to the fact that they are all the same.

In Latin America, there is probably an anti-market bias as a result of the Spanish Catholic culture, so opposite to commerce, and so friendly to the titles of nobility and privileges. There is where it lies its main cultural tie.

We can not escape despotism through marketing. It is not a question that the opponents of the despots hire a counselor to find out what people think of the any subject, to be able then to build adaptable candidatures. An honest debate is needed. It is curious to see what little importance is given to this honesty, in a reaction against profit, the sin is reduced to keeping with the money. However, when we speak of the ethics of the public policies, the intellectual dishonesty of marketing policies is not taken into account.

Luckily, the problem is not in charge of the politicians opposed to the despots. The debate includes those who do not need votes but attention. All kind of intellectuals, broadly speaking, participate- for good or bad, having influence on those who are less interested in public issues.

They are not attracted by an interest in surveys, they are only stuck to their image of "good people", which in a corrupt society is not particularly praised. It is there where changes must be operated.

Argentina, and I say this in pain, is a perfect bad example of this. In 1955, the Armed Forces destitute Juan Domingo Perón, who had used several of the false ideas herein exposed to build a great Fascist despotism.

The military government exchanged the Peronists for military people and two years later annulled the 1949 populist Constitution and sanctioned an amendment to the historical Constitution of 1853/60 which changed its proper nature by using expressions of wish such as "social rights".

It was then when Argentina operated the opposite to a miracle. Argentina is the only country which being a developed country turned into an underdeveloped. It is still a taboo to speak politically of something else than the false social-democrat benefits. There is such adherence to this formula that after some changes in the nineties, with the first problems, the country returned to the same old state vices, now with outstanding fanaticism.

Perhaps the conclusion might be summarized in: escaping from populism is not quitting its "evil" but its "goodness".

ABOUT THE AUTHOR

José Benegas is an Argentine lawyer, essayist and journalist. Master degree in Economics and Political Sciencies at "Concurso Caminos de la Libertad" (Aztec TV, Mexico), with honors. He is a member of the Interamerican Institute for Democracy Board. He has worked in radio, television and graphic media in many countries all over the world .

Other books by the same author on sale:

Hagase tu voluntad. Bajar del cielo para conseguir un cargador de iPhone (Unión Editorial, 2015)

Seamos Libres. Apuntes para volver a vivir en libertad (Unión Editorial, 2013)

La moral del violador. La ética del atraco como práctica política (Galileiland, 2014)

No me Parece. Los últimos meses de furia (Galileiland, 2014)

Escandalosa historia de amor (novela ética – Galileiland, 2013)